A PRESENT GOD - IN DEPRESSION

CHRISTA EDWARDS

authorHOUSE®

AuthorHouse™
1663 Liberty Drive
Bloomington, IN 47403
www.authorhouse.com
Phone: 1 (800) 839-8640

Published by AuthorHouse 12/17/2019

ISBN: 978-1-7283-3916-0 (sc)
ISBN: 978-1-7283-3915-3 (hc)
ISBN: 978-1-7283-3914-6 (e)

Library of Congress Control Number: 2019920575

Print information available on the last page.

CONTENTS

Foreword

The work of editing this book, A Present God – In depression has been both inspiring and encouraging, as well as being very insightful to me. It has been a profit and a blessing to my own soul allowing me to have a much better understanding and more loving concern for those who face depression on a daily or weekly bases. Christa has given some of her own experiences in this book which caused her to turn to Christ and in total surrender to Him, she has given all of her life's issues to His control. Her love for people, especially those who deal with depression, is shown in each chapter of her writing. It is my privilege to know the author well, and to know that her intention, in everything she wrote, was for the inspirational encouragement and salvation of her readers. May God bless it to many hearts, and may He use it for the uplifting and building of Christian character in the people who read it across this great country of Canada, and around the world.

Pastor Dennis King, Guelph, Ontario

Assistant Pastor, Kingdom Community International

FRONT COVER ART

This piece has been designed by Amber Edwards of Newfoundland. She is a 19-year-old aspiring artist. Her vision for artwork is undeniable, and her talent is a gift that God has certainly blessed her with. Amber has found art to be one of the most soothing ways to handle her depression and anxieties in her life. She is a very kind-hearted soul, who is learning her path in life, and doing so gracefully. She is an inspiration to so many people, and she loves God and is surely building a relationship with Him. I am so very humbled and blessed to say; She is my daughter; Whom I have shared with so many people, because her spirit is so beautiful, she needed extra people to help raise her, so that she could become the full potential of who she is. (I believe this fully, because hindsight is 20-20)! Our journey together has been a unique one, full of love, happiness and sadness at times. However, God is absolutely amazing, and He has brought her and I, through storms that we didn't even realize were happening until they were over. Time went so quickly. Now during this new season in Amber's life, God has something huge in store for her, as she walks beside Jesus, and puts her trust in Him, building that relationship before any other, she will see God move in ways indescribable through her life! Amber is a sunbeam in my life, she is such inspiration to me and in the lives of all those who are blessed to know her. Her depiction of this piece is as follows,

From the artists mouth:

What inspired me to create this drawing was my own depression and anxiety. My "monster" has long sharp nails that digs into my chest and it is a large dark thing that sits on my back and weighs me down. The light coming from the background represents God who is always and everywhere present, even in my darkest moments. I know that God will always protect me. He is bigger and brighter than my "monsters". He lights up my path in the times that I can't see in front of me, or what my future may hold.

-Amber Edwards

BACK COVER ART

This piece has been designed by Racheal Roche of Ontario. She is a 19-year-old who aspires to be a hair stylist, and then continue schooling into social work. In whatever she does, her life will touch the lives of many. Her vision for artwork is deep, and her talent is also a gift from God that I pray she uses to touch the lives of many. Racheal also used art as a way to handle her depression and anxieties in her life. Racheal, too, is a kind person and is trying to find her way in life, and I am also blessed to say that Racheal, is my niece and one of many family members that I have recently met for the first time. That, however, is another story, for another time. Racheal's depiction of the back-cover art piece is as follows,

From the artist's mouth:

The reason I chose to draw this piece, was because depression often weighs me down and makes me feel like I'm drowning. It's often hard to see the light when you are in such a deep, dark place. But when I can finally see light and break through the ocean of despair surface, I feel strong enough to actually let the light in, and I feel strong enough to be able to pull the weight up instead of letting it drag me under.

~ Racheal Roche

From the author;

Firstly, I want to address the elephant in the room, the multitude of different opinions, the multitude of different types of people, different backgrounds and beliefs of those that will read this manuscript. I want you all to know, that this book is based on my very personal, and very real experiences with God. Although you may believe differently than me, or think differently than me, if you are someone that is suffering with depression and anxiety, I hope that there will be something in this book that will help you with your journey in life. If you do not desire to hear about the miracles that God has done in my life, then I totally understand, and you don't need to read any further. However, if you are interested to see a different point of view, from someone who loves everyone, no matter their shape, color, size, background, sexual orientation, education, life status, or any other anomaly that you can insert in this list, by all means, read about my journey, about my eye opening. I want to share this because I love people, (the bible commands me to love my neighbor as myself – not just my Christian neighbors... ALL of my neighbors, and I do so with the Love of Jesus. I do not need to become political... I can just love people because they are all God's children, and they are all worthy of love and respect) and if my life and my story can be of some assistance in helping you or someone you love to be okay, if there is even a few words in this book that helps you see your depression differently, and gives you power over it, that is my goal, that is what is worth it for me to have exposed my experience, my soul and my life.

As you continue on the pages of this book, you will see a story unfold that is beautifully manifested through the wonderous works, and glory of God. God is good, merciful, loving and kind. I am tired of people forgetting that He exists, and I am tired of people thinking that God is so awful because He allows bad things to happen! Oh, how people are so very wrong. God is good, and just, God wants to correct this world, and the bible fully explains how He will do that, the reason He hasn't yet, is because He loves his people so much, everyone, and wants them all to choose the right path for their life. The right path for their eternity. Because God is not a dictator, that is why we are not forced to know Him, He awaits us with open arms. And it is the evil one that causes the evil in the world. God is there for our best interest in all situations. As you read this book through, may you experience Gods presence, and I hope that it sincerely helps you in your battle with depression and/or anxiety.

Please read this prayer, as it will help you understand the depths of this book.

First off, I want to say Thank You.

Thank you, God, for all of the blessings that you have placed on my life, for the wonderful treasures that you have blessed my life with. Each treasure has a name, of a friend, a family member, and the list goes on! You have blessed my life with incredible and loving people. Not just people who are related to me, but people from all walks of life, that have been introduced in order to lift me up! It was by Your Grace, and their help, that I have been able to receive a word from You Lord, that enables the blessings of the Holy Spirit's power and strength. Jesus, I thank you for taking the scales from my eyes, so that I can clearly see YOU. While I was in the world, living as a regular person, a sinner. I was so blind to your goodness and mercy, and how it truly does endure forever. Lord, you waited on me, while I tested the waters in the world, and You opened Your arms to me, when I returned to You even though I was tainted, tattered, bruised and beaten from the world's influence. Feeling unworthy and worthless, desolate and empty, not only have You picked up my broken pieces Lord, but You melted me down, as I prayed for, every porous hole in my soul to be filled, every hurt to be reversed, every blemish to be wiped clean. You filled my heart with joy, happiness beyond my ability to describe, and You did it, while I was at my lowest, weakest, saddest, and most depressed point in life. Jesus, people think that you work miracles like a magician, instant relief, instant healing, and instant change. Although you are more than capable of instant change, people forget that You are a long- suffering God, you often take your time in creating inward changes, and You do that for Your Glory, and for our benefit. The learning process in life is challenging, but You have so beautifully designed that process so that I could learn things that are so deep. I give You all of the praise, for taking Your time with me. Jesus, I pray that You will tear the scales from the eyes of everyone who reads this, that they will truly, openly see that they need You in their lives. I pray for every soul that reads this book, that they will experience your amazing presence. I thank You, Jesus, today for their life, for the wonderful gifts You have placed in them, and even if it is invisible to them right now, may they be assured that You are present in each and every situation they encounter in life. You are our Holy God, our Father in Heaven, hallowed be Your name, your kingdom come, may Your will be done on earth as it is in Heaven. Give us this day our daily bread. Forgive us Lord, as we forgive those who try to harm us, lead us not into temptation, but deliver us from evil, for Thine is the Kingdom, the power and the Glory, forever and forever, Amen.

I want to **DEDICATE** this book, **to the will of God** in my life, firstly. For without my life having a purpose, and without God showing me un-denying and everlasting love, I would have no reason to pursue in this path! I also dedicate this book to *my earthly father, Eugene*. Dad, you have been a rock for our family, you have fought in ways I can barely understand, because you love us. I am so thankful for your advice through the years, you may have thought many times that I wasn't listening, and you may have thought that it was never going to "sink in"… but I did listen, carefully, and I watched, intently. No one is perfect, and we all make mistakes, but as far as being an amazing father goes, you did a wonderful job. You raised me, as your own, and you had patience, when I didn't deserve it, you showed me care, when I was being less than nice as a child, and you taught me many lessons that helped me strive for greatness. For this I say thank you, and remind you, God isn't done with you yet. I also dedicate to *my Daughter, Amber*. You have endured plenty enough from the enemy. I pray that God will see you through each and every part of it. I know He will, if you give it all to Him. That is your personal choice. However, God is our ultimate protector, of heart, soul and mind. It is important that you never allow the enemy to win over you. The enemy will have no power where you close the door on him. You are my sunshine, I love you to the moon and back, to infinity. You are a light in the life of so many people! God has a special purpose and plan for your life. Listen closely to His still voice, so that you don't miss it. Because it's bigger than anything you will find for yourself. I thank you for being in my life, I thank God for blessing me with such an amazing daughter. Lastly, I dedicate to myself. I was burdened in ways I cannot describe; depression almost took me out, but God had a bigger purpose for my life. I could keep going, but those are the people that this book has been drawn from. It was birthed in the struggles that they, and I, have faced, and through the word of God and prayer have I found the answer to my question…. How do I finish this book? It wasn't until I realized it wasn't my story fully to be written but rather a guide for people lost like I was, and to be written to glorify God, not to self soothe. It is my hope and prayer, that, to anyone who reads it, this book will be a blessing to your life.

To the readers,

I could go on for pages of who I would love to thank for this book being written, but I can truly only thank, firstly, *My Heavenly Father*. For I have prayed, and it is only through Him that I can write these words. So, I thank God for blessing me with the content for which this book is written, from the words of wisdom, to the experiences that caused humble realities to set in. God really did turn it all around for good, and for His glory. Secondly, I want to thank *my sister, Vanessa*. She may not see herself in the light that I see her, but she inspires me to be better, in everything I do. But most importantly, she inspires me to be a better mother. She is an inspiration so vast that her light shone from the waters in Newfoundland and reached me in Alberta (when I lived there). I love you sis. From the days when we were playing in our front yard, to the special few moments of today. I wish I had not been selfish when I left home, for this I am eternally sorry. If I could go back to make positive changes, I would. I didn't think about the fact that you would be left alone, I was too excited to start my life. Oh, to go back and spend one more day playing Barbie's, as children, with you, or go for one more bike ride, as children, would be a glorious blessing. But, because our lives are in today and into the future, I will just be the best sister I can be, and the best aunt I can be to **Lauryn, Evan & Lydia**. They are treasures beyond measure. I admire your love and devotion to God, and to **your husband, Chris**. As I admire Chris's devotion also to God, to you and the kids. You are truly blessed! **My son, Alexander**, you are wise beyond your years, and are one of the kindest people I have ever had the pleasure of knowing, it is a joy to be your mom. Keep going forward with God, seek His face, and His will for your life. I know God has BIG plans for you! **To my mom**, thank you for believing in me. You have always been on my side and for this I am forever grateful. For all this and so much more. Thank you for listening, and caring. You are a wonderful person and I love you very much. A few other people that I have to thank, for reasons that are too vast to describe, for believing in me, for giving me hope in the darkest moments of my life and for standing by me through so much. I am forever grateful. **Tracy Gillingham. Denise and Peter Mwaiteleke. Pastor Dennis and Mary King. Albert Bodechon. Last but absolutely not least, Jesse B.** – My earthly counsellor. Thank you for listening to hours of renditions of my day/week, for listening to me cry, my animated antidotes when I was beyond stressed, for always looking happy to see me, when I felt like I should be hiding in a hole. You are an inspiration so much larger than you can ever imagine! You know who you are. And for all the ways you have spoken into my life to help me press forward, and the encouragement you offered to help me feel like myself again, I cannot thank you enough.

CHAPTER 1

LET IT BE

S o, when this book began, it had a completely different purpose. It had the purpose to be a revealing of struggles that I have endured in my life. It was intended to be an outlet for my own healing, and through the words being written, it would maybe touch the lives of other people. However. That was not the case. This is probably the fifth time I have started to write this book. And, I can tell you with 100% certainty, that this manuscript will become complete, simply because my writers block is gone, (that I've been in for months, by the way) God has opened my mind after filing it with all the words of the pages to follow. See, I understand that God will answer prayers, which is why each person should be careful what they pray for. The closer a person becomes to God, the more we learn to understand how He works in our lives. For example, if you pray that God will grant patience. That is the BRAVEST thing you can pray for... you may ask, why? I'll tell you. Think about it, what is the situation surrounding you when you lose your patience? Usually chaos of some kind... a child repeatedly asking for food, or water, or to go outside, or to play etc.... a boss consistently telling you how to fold the napkin when ... "UGH! ITS JUST A NAPKIN! I KNOW HOW, BACK OFF", bursts from your mouth. Driving in traffic and seeing other drivers being reckless, or too slow, or inconsiderate. How about standing in line up at the grocery store? I'm sure that is something of a patience tester. But thankfully, God has a beautiful formula for teaching us the lessons in life that we need to learn, and placing us in situations that demand our patience, is a way that we will learn to have more of it. Now that I have sufficiently elaborated on that... here is what you *need* to understand. I had been praying for help, praying for a clean heart, a clean mind and spirit. Drawing closer and closer to God and feeling His Holy presence around me. I could go back into my sordid past and explain how profound this reality is, however, as I said, this is not my book, this is a book written to glorify God, so all you need to know at this moment is this. I have walked in the world; I was involved in things that were very ungodly, there is very little of the world that you can think of, that I have not done or been a part of, or entertained. I am not proud of this, I am embarrassed to admit it, but in order for you to understand that my life is a testimony, you need to know some of the details. I will write that book someday, God willing. However, I now have the blessing and peace that He brings, thanks to his mercy and grace on my life since my repentance of sin. I can not thank God enough, for making me whole. It is an experience that is so deep, and transformational, it is very difficult to explain.

Now, even I didn't see this coming. I CANNOT stress to you enough; I absolutely did not see it approaching my life... I was FULLY blindsided to what happened next that started me on the path of revelation to how my writers block would finally be lifted. See, God takes his time. He wants to get it right for us, just as our fathers or mothers want to do something right for us when we, as their children, ask. Our Heavenly Father takes our requests seriously. He works to make the ideal circumstances for us to receive our blessing. But we, must also be obedient, and willing. Open hearted and earnestly seeking after God. Building our relationship with him daily.

So, on July 31, 2019 (yep, that recent!), I woke up from sleeping… nothing particular on my mind, nothing really stressful (Thanks be to God), and no real agenda for the day other than to work on the computer. I did the normal thing, (before I even put on my glasses, or got up from the bed) I grabbed my phone, peeked at Facebook, and then suddenly, as if someone completely took me over, I felt a warm wave of love flow over me, and God spoke to my soul, and I listened. I barely stopped typing until it was done, and while I was typing, I was in disbelief at the speed at which I typed (on a cell phone, thumb typing... come on, you all know what I mean, that should normally, be fairly slow, but my thumbs moved so fast and I had no time to think!) I ended up with a very LONG prayer written in my phone… this prayer was not intended for me, this prayer was intended for someone close to me that needed it, at that very moment. I knew the person for which it was intended because God placed a vision of only his face in my mind while I wrote.

I can tell you, the one moment that I did stop typing and took a breath, I looked to my Bible, and when I turned the pages, I wasn't in one of the books of the Bible, no, I was in the dictionary section, in the back. And the page that I was on, had a verse reference under the word Devil - (I didn't notice the location of the verse until after I was done writing and praying) what I was drawn to, was this: JAS 4-7. For you to understand fully the power of this, I must first admit, when I read the Bible, normally I will go to my favorite chapters. Psalms or Proverbs. I have read the book of Job, and random verses of other books. But I can truthfully say, that the book of Proverbs is my main go to. So, when I saw the letters JAS, my first thought was, what book is that? I couldn't even think of the name. Thanks be to God, my Bible has tabs on the sides with the three letter acronyms to distinguish the books of the Bible, so I looked, and found that JAS was actually the acronym to the Book of James.

A book that I never think of, that I've never taken any time to read. However, when I read the words, I knew one million percent that this was God's guidance, for the verse read like this: NLT - James 4 verse 7 & 8 "so humble yourselves before God. Resist the devil, and he will flee from you. Come close to God, and God will come close to you. Wash your hands, you sinners; purify your hearts, for your loyalty is divided between God and the world." In this God spoke to me and said, "write this". As I continued to read, the next verse (verse 9) says, "Let there be tears for what you have done. Let there be sorrow and deep grief. Let there be a sadness instead of laughter, and gloom instead of Joy." And God spoke to my heart and said, "do not write that". And as I continued to read verse 10 "Humble yourselves before the Lord, and he will lift you up in honor." And God spoke again, "write that", and in that instant, I went back to writing. I wrote as He had spoken to my heart. I didn't understand it at the time, it was so surreal. When I finished the prayer, I became overwhelmed with emotion. I prayed over the prayer before I sent it. Because I want to do the will of God, and only the will of God, in everything I do in life. As a human, the devil tries to manipulate our thoughts, and wants us, to NOT believe that it's real. The devil is the ultimate narcissist, but I know the truth. Because I experienced the deep joy of the revelation of God in my spirit. God spoke so clearly to me, and for His glory ONLY, I sent the message. I was clear to say that these words were not of me, they were from God to the intended recipient. Now, to step back, after sending the message, I read what was written. Keep in mind, I hadn't written anything significant in months, because each blank screen, each blank piece of paper was screaming at me an echo of nothingness. I was wracking my brain to put words to paper but getting nothing. I felt like I had a completely useless and empty brain. It wasn't until this moment, when the prayer was done, that it hit me like a ton of bricks, my gift as a writer comes from the grace of God. I wasn't intended to be a writer of worldly things, my calling is to write in such a way as to speak to the hearts of people, through the words that only GOD can provide. The reason my brain felt empty was because God had been spending months working on me, and clearing my mind of all the bad, unnecessary and worldly things. (No wonder I felt like I had nothing left in my head to write from), God was preparing my renewed mind to be a space that was big enough to receive the words that He wanted me to write. And so, my writers block was lifted. Praise be to God.

Again, stepping back to the verse in the Bible that was included in the prayer. When I read the prayer through, I noticed heavily, what God said after the verse was placed. (Please remember, the word which God spoke, was a prayer, that this individual **needed** to pray, God provided the words for the individual, so that he would know how to pray for healing in his spirit and healing in his mind from depression.) And so, the words written after the Bible verses read: "Father God, I thank you this day, at this moment, for knowing I have suffered much and that I need you, Father God, for you are holy and patient." And God spoke again to me, again, a revelation like a ton of bricks. God didn't want me to include the verse 9 of James chapter 4 because the intended recipient of this particular prayer, had already endured enough emotional suffering, pain and tears. And it was not the intention for God, to make him feel that he was due more pain, but instead he was due healing, if he obeys and prays the prayer God had provided. Since the recipient, has been out of words, not knowing where to turn in his life, or in his mind, but God knows all circumstances. He heard the cries from the soul of this person that needed to get the words to pray, and God gave me the blessing to pass that prayer on to him. When I was done writing, I was in shock, awe and utter astonishment. Again, I first prayed over the prayer before sending it, and then I cried for the overwhelming joy that I felt in my soul, knowing that I heard and I listened and obeyed what God asked of me.

Unknown to me at that time, the person who received the prayer, was going through a horrible morning with Depression (it was later reported to me by someone close to him). This person did not expect, especially from me, a prayer that God granted him, the words he was lacking, to pray to God, for his depression. I am unaware, to this day, if he actually prayed that prayer - however, that is between him and God. I pray always for his deliverance from depression. To God be all the glory! God works in beautiful and wonderful ways, and it is by faith that I can say I believe that Jesus died for me, He rose from the dead for me, He won the battle over Satan, hell, and the grave. Jesus is alive and our heavenly Father LOVES us! God is present with us, every day, every moment, through every sadness, every failure and trouble. God has been with me through many trials and tribulations, some I had even created for myself with my own bad decisions, bad choices, and then turned around and wondered, why are bad things were happening in my life? It's amazing to me, that when you step out of darkness and into the light that Jesus provides, how differently we can see the world and others around us. It's amazing, and beautiful, and my prayer is that every person on the face of this earth could enjoy the beauty that it brings within. Many people feel that God is "old", that He isn't present in today's world because the world has become so "modernized", that miracles don't happen anymore, because miracles are only in stories of the Bible from the days of old. People are blinded to so much, and I was among the blind, leading the blind. I was among the unaware and walking in the deepest darkness. I came from depths of depression so vast, that I almost believed that Satan himself, created me, and not God. Because I felt like such a horrible wretched person for so long. I FELT that way, (key component here, my feelings weren't created from the good things people said to me, they were from the mean comments, and the dark words used to describe me when I had failed in life. I wasn't a good enough mom, I wasn't worthy, I wasn't successful enough, I was selfish, I didn't look good enough, etc.) I started saying these things to myself after some time as well. Some of the people that personally know me, would think to themselves, (and might text me to say), there's no way that someone would say that stuff to you! But, let me tell you, it isn't always in the exact words, it's in how you treat a person. It's in the sideway looks, the "I'm better than you, because I have more attitude". The words that we speak and the tone of our voice, do highly affect how a person feels about themselves. I stopped looking people in the eye because I was afraid that they would see me for how I saw myself... I hated myself, and I didn't want to be hated by them. I was in the world, and I forgot that God saw all of me, every emotion, every thought, and every detail. He doesn't miss a heartbeat. I do not have to hang my head in shame any longer, Praise be to God!

The devil uses people who are not close to God, and some who are religious, but not those in relationship with Jesus, to tear us down, to eat at our self-worth, to play with the mind and further rot the emotional brain that we have. Depression starts to set in when, we ourselves, allow other people's negative opinions control our thinking for things that have happened to us. It gets inside of us, instead of dealing with it on the outside of us! And usually, we hold unto a fear that people will mock us, or make us feel less than good enough, if we let out the truth of how or what we feel. The Devil is a trickster, he is a monster that hides behind masks and he is a liar. He will present himself to you as someone you don't find to be harmful. "Yes, I'll go to that wild party, I know there will be drugs there, but I can stay away from it", then you get to the party (as an example), and the most attractive person to you walks up, puts their arm around you and compliments you... then offers to get you a drink. Then before the night ends, you're in bed with this person, not fully aware of what's happening, and suddenly the person is pregnant, or you are pregnant, or you have contracted a disease of some sort. Suddenly, you hear yourself saying, why is this happening to me? I was so stupid; I was so dumb.

Stop talking to yourself like that. The devil will use our own negativities about ourselves against us every time!

No matter what the Devil does to trick us, to cause us to be in strange and unusual situations and no matter what decisions you have made for yourself, do not call yourself names. Tearing yourself down will be the seeds that the Devil uses to manipulate your mind, to tear harder at your heart, to pull you further from the truth, and further from God and His Word, The Bible. The seeds of depression often start when we are young, and we tell ourselves the wrong things, we listen to the wrong voices in our life, we forget to seek good things. If we fill our mind with the Word of God and good thoughts, we will grow seeds of goodness in our souls. It is important for you to understand that depression is not a sin, although it comes from the Devil. Jesus even said at one point, in the Garden of Gethsemane in NLT- Mark 14: 34 "He told them (the disciples), "my soul is crushed with grief to the point of death. Stay here and keep watch with me". Verse 35 - He went on a little farther and fell to the ground. He prayed that, if it were possible, may the awful hour awaiting him might pass him by." Verse 36, "Abba Father" He cried out, "everything is possible for you. Please take this cup of suffering away from me, yet I want your will to be done, not mine." Jesus took it to God, in prayer. He expressed in agony to His Heavenly Father that He didn't want to endure this depression, and what was about to come upon Him (dying on the cross).

Overall, Jesus wanted the will of GOD to be done in His life, regardless of the season of anguish He had to endure in order to have His Father's purpose fulfilled. It was His purpose that brought him through His depression, and it was also His purpose that broke the power of depression. God received the glory in both. Jesus' prayer in the Garden of Gethsemane that dark night, was answered by His Father by sending angels to strengthen Him. Jesus died, therefore his suffering ended, and all worked together for the Glory of God, and He did it all, to save mankind. People, humans who question, and mock and scorn God and Jesus. Yes, I know the question, how is it that, Jesus could be tainted by depression if it comes from the Devil?

While Jesus walked the earth among us, the Devil tempted Jesus, because he had not yet defeated him in the grave, and the devil had reason to try and break Jesus, just as he tries to break humans. Jesus had to endure the human experience so that he could save us.

I am a Christian, but I used to be a religious Christian (yes, there is a difference) when I was growing up. As I became a teenager and young adult, I was starting to see a difference, and see how Good God really is, but at the same time, reading the Bible, going to church, praying… all felt like tasks that had to be completed. Like duties of the day, household chores. It didn't feel like something I wanted to do. It felt more like something I had to do. And when you look at your prayer life and your Christian walk as a chore, well, let's just say, you are in a complacent place, where the Devil has great opportunity to come into your mind and to manipulate you into believing that you can "just try it", and "your still a Christian, even if you're involved in this or that", Satan has a way of twisting our mindset to distract us from our purpose and destiny. Before we know it, we're doing things that does not, in any way, glorify God. At the end of the day, if we are giving our time and attention to something or someone that takes away from our prayer life, and from our devotion to God, we are putting a wedge between Him and our hearts. Now, this doesn't mean that you stop everything in your life (quit your job, stop talking to people, etc.) to focus 100% on God. No, Instead, if you decide to put your 100% focus on God, including Him in everything in your life, that is where you will see a beautiful transformation. It may take some time, but it is well worth your time and effort!

Again I will take you to the example of a relationship… when you fall in love with someone, you desire to spend your time with them, to talk to them, and when you are at work, you include their name in conversation, when you are among friends, you include their name someway in conversation. No matter what your day consists of, your mind will drift to that person you are in a relationship with. Now, imagine if your focus on God was of the same intensity. God would be first in your heart and life, and in the middle of your earthly relationships. How beautiful that life is.

CHAPTER 2

WHERE IS GOD?

S o many people, especially new Christians, often wonder "Where is God?"

You may be one of these people. You were at church, and the pastor delivered an anointed sermon that spoke to your heart in a profound way. Then at some point during the service, the pastor made an alter call, for anyone that wanted to receive Christ as their personal savior. Your feeling convicted and want to respond while the adrenaline is running high, sweat has formed on your brow. (possibly in the armpits, and even chest and back, which just makes you more self-conscious), but you take the step to go forward to have the pastor, or one of the prayer team members to pray with you while you invite Jesus into your heart. There is much rejoicing, and you feel so good in your soul and your spirit, with a true sense of joy and peace. You go home and the Devil tries to seal it from you, and you feel like nothing has changed.

Your husband or wife is still a frustration to your life in many ways, your children are still not doing as they are told, and they challenge your patience, before becoming a follower of Jesus, you used to use profanity as an outlet. But now, you try to stop your tongue as a word slips out in anger. Suddenly you get this feeling that maybe you're not good enough to be a Christian because you can't seem to stop speaking profanity, or maybe your anger is still there, or maybe you still crave that cigarette, or that bottle, or that sex partner, or whatever unhealthy habit you had in your life. Maybe, you're in the midst of it, this very moment. You start to feel that insufficient feeling in your chest, and your mind becomes clouded with thoughts that you can't give up your addiction. But your heart wants what it felt on Sunday at church, and you start to question. Where is God? Why haven't you fixed all of these problems for me? God, why do I feel depressed and Sad? God, I thought you were going to take all the bad habits out of my life.

There are so many things that we say to God in secret, that we may not admit to anyone in life. There are things we question, and we end up chasing ourselves in circles. It's amazing how we allow the enemy, the Devil, to just have his way with our hearts and our minds, when we should just do as Jesus told us to do, rebuke the devil, in His name, and He will flee from you. Jesus told us to use the authority of HIS NAME, when dealing with Satan and demons.

Here is the reality, when we pray that prayer, asking Jesus to come into our heart, asking God to come into our life, each soul, yourself included, need to understand that God is not a genie. He is not going to grant you wishes. He isn't going to grant you, every desire in life. But I'll tell you what he will do for you, if you have patience, and you desire this with an honest heart, and you want God in your heart and in control of you. (Yes, it is hard to let go of control, but it is possible, even for the most stubborn, and while I type the words, I see my own face, since I was so very stubborn.)

God will transform you; He will work with the bad and turn it to good, He will give you the tools you need to fix your bad situations, your hurts, your sadness, your depression and anxiety. God never intended for His children to endure these things. Our reality is that we have invited those things in from the moment we allow the Devil to take control of our thoughts. God will walk with you and be your comfort and your peace, if you let Him. The key to this, is LETTING GOD DO HIS JOB! Stop expecting immediate results, and do as God has asked, seek His face and not His hands, meaning keep your heart in the right place, instead expecting material things. Pray. Pray diligently, every day, and THANK GOD for what he has given you in life, and for divine protection over you, bringing you safely this far in life. Praise God for what He has done in your life and for the destiny that he has planned for you as in Jeremiah 29:11. And make sure, to read verse 12, 13 & 14 as well. Because in there is the instruction, and the desire of God's heart, for you to obey, in order for verse 11 to become your utmost reality.

You may ask, where is God? But God is asking, where are you, my child? His desire is for us to love Him, give Him worship and praise. Some people may challenge this and say that God is selfish, but just look at yourself in a relationship… do you not enjoy it, when your spouse praises you? When your spouse thanks you for your hard work and dedication to the relationship? Think about it. God wants our praise, and worship, and rightfully so, for if it wasn't for Him, we wouldn't exist. And if it wasn't for His mercy and grace, and sending His Son, Jesus Christ, to earth to die for our sins, we wouldn't have any hope or a future.

God is in our past, even in the bleakest moments, if you really look, you can see Him. He's the opportunity you turned down because you didn't feel good enough, He's in the person you didn't talk to because you didn't feel confidence, He's in the moments that you felt you couldn't go on... but YOU are still here. Remember, God is always out for your best interest.

God is PRESENT in our lives, in our past, our current situation and our futures. God goes before us to make a way, as he has given us the right to make decisions for ourselves, but as believers, children of God, when we make the wrong decision, God is there to redirect us, to help us and guide us, and He will do so, diligently and with utmost care, if we seek after Him. God sent Jesus, His son, to die on the cross for us, there is no greater love than this.

John 17:1-4 After saying all these things, Jesus looked up to heaven and said, "Father, the hour has come. Glorify Your son, so He can give glory back to You. For You have given Him authority over everyone. He gives eternal life to each one, who have received Christ by faith. And this is the way to have eternal life – to know You, the only true God, and Jesus Christ, the one you sent to earth. I brought glory to You here on earth by completing the work You gave me to do. Now, Father bring me into the glory we shared before the world began." This was the final prayer of Jesus. Jesus gave His life, so that we may not die, but instead, we get to live.

Live on this earth to glorify God so that we can truly LIVE in heaven! This is good news! Wonderful news! And everyone on the earth, there is extended a welcome to come into fellowship with God, all that a person has to do, is repent and believe.

Through faith you will see life change before your eyes. You will ask me, how do you know, you are just reading scripture. I know, because I was a sinner, a person who swore, a person who mocked, laughed, danced, partied, partook in less than graceful activities, smoked cigarettes (a lot) and although I was a kind hearted person, I wasn't anything of who I am today. My story is a long and detailed one, and maybe someday, God will grant me the blessing to write that book, as previously mentioned. The one this was originally intended to be. But for now, I will say this. I was a sinner, I was unclean in the spirit, and I found my way to JESUS, NOT to religion, not to rules and regulations, to JESUS. And when you find your way to Jesus, you are filled with the Holy Spirit, you are filled with a joy so deep that even the worst days are bearable. You have no desire, no need, no want to be a part of anything in the world. No one has to say, "you're not supposed to do that", because the blood of Jesus, and the Grace of GOD will take away your desires for earthly things. It may not happen all in one moment, day or a year, but as you seek God, once you get a taste of the joy and happiness only He can bring, you continue seeking after Him, and it is in your desire to know Him better, that the transformation takes place, and it will continue. Suddenly your coworkers will be asking why you are so happy when you were once so sad, and why you can smile even in terrible tribulations, but that's the beauty of God's Grace. He understands our humanity. God will give life, hope and a future, if you seek Him in spirit and in truth.

I smoked cigarettes for a few days after giving my heart to God, but my desire to be close to God was REAL, and my desire to know Christ and feel His love in my life was so strong, my prayers were diligent and true, so God took my desire to smoke away. From that moment, not only did I not crave it anymore, I didn't suffer the coughing fits, I didn't feel the pang of desire ever again. It's almost been a year... and God has totally delivered me from it, unscathed, because I had faith that He would deliver me.

I have been around smokers; I have smelled it. It does nothing for me anymore. There is no desire there and for that I can only thank, my Almighty Heavenly Father. I was a smoker for years and years, and at the point of my conversion I was smoking over

2 packs of cigarettes a day. Those who knew me as a smoker, know that I smoked a lot, and I used to profess that it was my "one bad thing". Guess what. I do not desire it or any bad thing anymore. If God could minister to my heart and deliver me from what I was in, He can surely deliver you. When we speak of becoming a Christian, we speak of being born again. Most people don't understand what that really means. Think about it… what happens when a child is born into the world? They are delivered.

Jesus died, so that we might be delivered from sin. When we confess our sins to Him, we receive within us the Spirit of God, and our spirit bare witness with His spirit that we are born again, made new in the spirit of the inner man or woman. I know this is true, and it is profound. Because God is the creator of all things, and we are created in His image, it is through Him that our flesh and bones inside our mother's womb develop into a human body, with a soul and a spirit. When we are born, we are born in sin, due to the fall of Adam and Eve recorded in Genesis. We are raised from birth, we are born sinners, and if we are raised in the church, or not. If raised in a Christian home and we fall away from God's will… whatever the circumstance, our reality is that there comes an age of responsibility, and if we choose to just lead our own path, and deny God the ability to do His divine Will in our life, then we have continued against the Will of God. God has declared to all mankind through his Son, Jesus Christ, that we have an opportunity to be delivered from sin, to be born again, in the spirit through Him. I know this to be true, because I've experienced it personally. I AM born again in the spirit. And you don't have to take my word for it. I have a multitude of family and friends who knew me before now, some for all of my life, some for part of my life, and I believe all of them would say, that this woman is the same kindhearted person, but has a new spirit, there's something different about her! I have told them, and I will tell you, the difference, is Jesus. Jesus offers life and life more abundantly. He declared, I am the way, the truth and the life and no one comes to the Father, but through me.

So, to get back to the question, where is God? God is waiting on us to make the decision to seek Him. See, God is not a dictator, He will never force His hand while we are under grace. He allows all people to have a choice in the life they want.

However, people still blame God when bad things happen. Most people do not realize or think about the day Jesus was crucified. Jesus stripes, the whip marks on His back, they represent all the sickness in the world. He bled for us, because He knew the evil that was fighting against us. When Jesus died on the cross, He gave us an opportunity to escape hell. God doesn't want the bad things that are happening, Satan is the father of evil. God has already stated, in the bible, that He would end all evil on this earth. He will do so when He returns to bring his people home. However, He waits, He is longsuffering, because Jesus loves us so much, He gives us chance after chance, when we only curse His name, and say He doesn't exist, to open our eyes and open our hearts. He doesn't want to see us suffer, but if that is what we choose for ourselves, on the day of revelation, we will have no one but ourselves to blame. God is here, and He waits for you, and just like any other relationship... you will only get out of it, what you put in it. If you want it to work, you have to work at it and show your dedication and love. Because God will be showing his dedication and love to you. Even in the darkest moments of life.

CHAPTER 3

WHERE DO I FIT IN?

An age-old question, is, where do I fit in? I have asked myself this question, even recently. And I don't know even now, exactly where I fit in. But as I continue in prayer, and I seek the face of God, and my desire to be close to my heavenly Father, I am starting to see the revelation in my life of how God is answering my questions. And the question, where do I fit in? Is being answered in pieces. I am seeing my world and my life in such a different light. I have come to realize that I scrambled after people always. I had many, many, many "friends", and I was ALWAYS constantly checking in on them. Texting, or calling, inviting them to dinner, making food for them, entertaining them. It was exhausting, but now I have taken a good step back, looked at everything, and realized that I was chasing after people who were not in turn, chasing after me. So, I abruptly stopped, texting, calling and checking in. My phone went dead silent, for about two days. Then a few people checked in on me to see how I was doing, because they noticed I wasn't online and noticed that I was quiet. Many others, to this day, I still have them programmed in my phone, but have never once taken a moment to text me and say, "hi", How have you been doing? Not once. This taught me such a profound lesson. That we are sometimes taken advantage of, but only because we are the one offering up the advantage. We want to have people in our lives that want to be there, that love us, and enjoy our friendship. We don't want people in our lives that just want something from us all the time and never give anything in return, Right? (For the sticklers (sticklers = critics) … yes, I know you exist! Anything = not always stuff, or physical things, but emotional kindness and support.)

The same is for God. He desires us to chase after him, but He is also chasing after us. I like the words to this song, Reckless

Love by Cory Asbury, "There's no shadow You won't light up, Mountain You won't climb up, Coming after me, There's no wall You won't kick down, Lie you won't tear down, Coming after me." God always wants our attention, love and praise, and our gratefulness for the blessings that He bestows on our lives. It is a warranted desire. Not that God needs to prove anything to us, but He does anyway. Because we are human, and we are not God. God is all knowing, and kind and just. Humans are untrusting, unsure, and doubtful.

Where do we fit in? We fit in with the will and desire of God for our lives. If you truly chase after God, and truly desire to know him, He will help you through all of the muck that you have to crawl through, just to get yourself free from the clutches of the Devil on your life. Don't forget, God has already won. You can shout that from the rooftops of your homes! Devil, you are not welcome in this place, God is the Lord of this house and you are already defeated, so take your evil demons of doubt, and evil demons of depression and anxiety, demons of anger and frustration, and get out of my home and my family... and my life. Repeat it every time the Devil attacks, be stern, and intentional in your actions.

On a human level, where do we fit in? We fit where we seek. If we seek after evil things, places that are dark, and lonely, that is where we will find our place, but although we may fit in, we will not feel peace and comfort. If we seek after goodness and mercy, and seek after God, we will fit in with people who love Jesus. We will find a family of people who love God, and care for people. Where you fit in will largely depend on who you are as a person, and who you want to be as a person. The choice will always be yours. God doesn't force us to follow him, but he desires that we all follow him. He wants our love and admiration, but he will never force you to give Him anything, He gives us everything, right down to the breath we breathe. He will stand at your heart, knocking, and desiring to be close to you, but He will never force Himself in. See, Jesus is light. He claimed in scripture, I am the light of the world. No evil can survive in the light for light dispels darkness.

No depression can survive inside of you, when you have Jesus at the top of your priority list. No anxiety can consume you, when you have God protecting your heart and mind. Yes, changes take time, and as humans we will face sadness, that is a normal human emotion. But depression, the crippling pain that comes from it, the mind-numbing blankness that comes from it, and the demonic power that it holds over you, that is what absolutely cannot survive in you forever, if you put Christ first in your life. He will clear out your darkness if you seek after Him. Because depression is a gift of the Devil, and he loves to see souls swirling in depths of discontentment, insanity, desperation, and despair, thinking that no one loves them, no one cares, no one desires their presence, that they are always in the way, that they are a nuisance and the world is better without them.

He puts a heavy weight on the souls that suffer from depression. Makes them feel powerless to fight against a huge force holding them down, when all they want to do is get up and be happy. The Devil enjoys torturing the souls of God's people when we aren't close enough to God. He also enjoys tightening the chest, making you feel like you are sinking when people are too close, making you lose your breath, when faced with the smallest of situations. Giving you the feeling that you are going to have a heart attack, all the symptoms there, except the actual heart attack itself. It's a reality. I can attest this to be true. Because I was suffering with depression and anxiety. The deep kind that kept me in bed for days.

The crippling grip of evil emotions that made me feel not good enough… and the anxiety that overtook me when I had to go out in public was atrocious! Me, the woman who had placed second in speak off competitions. Me, the woman who could draw a crowd together and pull off some of the biggest parties. ME, the woman who was always smiling. Me, the woman who everyone always complimented that was such a great inspiration to them. Me. And I was depressed. I was under the veil of the Devils lies.

He swarmed me with darkness and put me in a pit of spiraling emotions so deep that I was going to commit suicide because I felt the world was better off without me. My children were better off without me. It was in my darkest, saddest, and deepest moment that there was a glimmer of light. It was so small, but so very significant. And it was in that moment that

I gave my life to the Lord. I was alone, and I was in it so deep. But I gave it up to God.

The depression didn't go away instantly, however in that moment, I could feel myself rising from the depth I was in. The thought of suicide left me. But the depression was still there. But I prayed. Honestly, and earnestly for a long time. I gave my life to Christ in November of 2018, and I felt my depression and anxiety finally fully release from me about the beginning of July 2019. The Devil never wants anyone to leave is kingdom of darkness and join Christ Kingdom of light. He holds deep in our soul and doesn't let go easily. He will fight for our souls because he enjoys the torturous grip that he has, but Christ will provide strength for us. He will follow through. There are sometimes that He allows the battle to go long. Not because He doesn't love us, but because He wants us to be truly earnest in our desires. There is a quote that you can place on your door that will help you keep this in mind,

"You are one decision away from a totally different life". – Mark Batteron.

Think about it. If I prayed for depression to go away, and it left me immediately (which is within God's power to do, and He does do for some), I would never have been given the blessing of developing my spiritual life and strengthening my soul. God knew my heart back then, and He knew that if He gave me instant gratification, that I would never get to the place emotionally, in my relationship with Him that I am today. I had to pray and draw close to God over the months of what, I now call, the healing process. The Devil had done a number on my soul, emotions, mind and spirit, and God took His time, because He wanted to make me whole again, in the right time, but in such a way that I would always acknowledge his greatness, and thank Him for His mercy in my life.

God is good. All the time, every day and in every way. I am a child of God; I am a Christian and I stand by the promises in the Bible, God's living Word. Through my walk with God, I no longer need to fit in anywhere in an earthly sense, because I fit in with God. And if the maker of the universe isn't embarrassed to be associated with a person like me, then no one else's opinion of me really matters. I thank God for his grace. His mercy endures forever. I love this quote by Zig Ziglar, when obstacles arise, you change your direction to reach your goal, you do not change your decision to get there.

CHAPTER 4

IN THE STORM

Each of us endures a storm at one time or another in our lives. These storms are often very stressful and strenuous times for us. In this particular one, I am talking about the storm of depression and anxiety. If you have received Jesus as your Lord and Savior, there is a good chance that you feel as though depression and anxiety should not be a part of your life. You are absolutely right! God does not intend for us to worry or carry any type of depression or anxiety. To know this, all we have to do is look at some scripture. (NLT)

Deuteronomy 31:8: The LORD himself goes before you and will be with you; He will never leave you nor forsake you. Do not be afraid; do not be discouraged."

Psalm 34:17: The righteous cry out, and the LORD hears them; he delivers them from all their troubles.

Psalm 40:1-3: I waited patiently for the LORD; turned to me and heard my cry. (2) He lifted me out of the slimy pit, out of the mud and mire; he set my feet on a rock and gave me a firm place to stand. (3) He put a new song in my mouth, a hymn of praise to our God. Many will see and fear the LORD and put their trust in him.

Psalm 3:3: But you, LORD, are a shield around me, my glory, the one who lifts my head high.

Psalm 42:11: Why, my soul, are you downcast? Why so disturbed within me? Put your hope in GOD, for I will yet praise him, my Savior and my God. If you are new to scripture, or if you are new to the Bible in general, the Book of Psalms was written mostly by King David of Israel.

Something that a lot of people do not notice about the Book of Psalms, is that King David was depressed, and had a heavy heart. And had to, many times, self soothe in order to overcome his feelings. Go back and read Psalm 42:11 again... King David is talking to himself, as he does in many of the Psalms. Why do you think that is? Do you think God had forsaken him? Absolutely not. God is with King David. However, God has commanded us that we have faith and believe in Him. King David had to endure things in his life, as we all do, but because he was seeking after God, it kept him close to his relationship with God, and that would give him a reason to stay humble.

Depression is not meant as a means to make you humble, depression is from the Devil, whose plan is to break you and keep you from the presence of God. But God takes the bad things in our lives and uses them for his Glory. He took King David's depression, and used it as a blessing to so many nations.

The Psalms that David wrote, has blessed many people in every generation. The Bible doesn't actually use the word "depression" anywhere in the King James Version, but it does give guidance to deep grief, and turmoil. See, God doesn't leave us or forsake us, but we do have to seek after him with an open, honest and earnest heart. Again, and I will repeat this through this book, but when God is making changes in us, He won't always make it instantaneous. Where is the faith in that? How much faith would a person have, or even need to have, if every time they prayed God acted like a genie and went "Poof here's what you need", "Poof, here's what you need."

If God acted like a genie, He would be just adhering to our desires, giving the blessings instantly, and then what use would we have for God? He would be useless to us. God desires us to honor Him for his blessings. We have to be in a place of humbleness, a gentle place full of emotion, that is poured out in our honor and love for God, THANKING HIM for all of the blessings we currently have in our lives and praying in FAITH, SPIRIT AND TRUTH that God will answer our prayers.

We may have to pray a million times before the miracle comes, I guess it depends on the condition of your relationship with God. Let's imagine your relationship with God equaled the messiness of a human divorce. The reconciling with your spouse, and you having to learn to trust and receive from your spouse again, that would, without a doubt, be full of trials and it might take some time and a long emotional process. But if you simply had a fight, or made a mistake, and immediately asked forgiveness, it may be a little quicker to get past and you would much more easily pour out your love and blessings for your spouse again... right?

The same is in our relationship with God. Again, open your eyes and your minds and see that God is good, just, kind and longsuffering. He has put up with us slandering his name, cursing, harming our bodies, living in infidelity, lying to ourselves and to others, using our words to damage others, spitting on those "below" us instead of reaching back and pulling them forward, and the list goes on.

If any of us had someone treating us this way, going against all the goodness we were trying to bestow on someone... as a human, we would probably lose patience. God is God for a reason! He is almighty, and all knowing. He sees us in our walk ... and He is always trying to bring us into a relationship with Him, but he allows us the choice to do as we please and desire. Although what we please and desire (multiple sex partners, heavy drinking, drug abuse, all night parties while the kids put themselves to bed, and the list goes on and on) to do can be devastating to our lives, and in the devastation, we like to lay blame and place blame. (example: Our teen kids don't respect us, it's those video games, tv shows... ask yourself, what did you do as a parent to warrant the respect? Did you teach them about the dangers of filling their minds with evil from a young age? Did you monitor what they were watching? What they were involved in?) We blame, usually where it doesn't belong. Here is another great quote. "You will get all you want in life, if you help enough other people get what they want." - Zig Ziglar

God will take the condition of the relationship that you have with Him, and work though the trials, He will teach us how to learn to love and trust again. But the key, is within our own selves. This is an amazing quote, "What lies behind us and what lies in front of us are tiny matters compare to what lies inside of us." – Henry Stanly Haskins. We have to know that it is up to us to go to God, ask for forgiveness, seek after him with a humble heart, and know that He is GOD. He is loving and the relationship we have with Him, no matter how muddled we see it to be, can be restored. The same as in a marriage.

If two people, even if they are far from each other emotionally, and have slandered, and harmed and hurt the other. (For clarification, God does not slander us, but is far from us if we are seeking the ways of the world), but if those two people, come together genuinely, and with the desire in BOTH their hearts to reconcile, the marriage can be made whole again. So, if you seek after God, with a genuine desire to be made new, your relationship with God can be restored, and in that, God will begin to heal the sadness, depression, and pain you feel in your soul. Sometimes God does give us instant blessings of healing, sometimes He takes his time, let God's will be done.

We should know, as people of God, that He is all powerful, and capable of healing us all in the right way, in the right time, for the right reasons. He sees our lives and has a plan for each of us. Our lives are His masterpiece. If He cares for the sparrows, He will surely care for us.

God has blessed these words, please take them to heart, and apply them properly to your life. I pray that something that I have said in this has blessed you, inspired you or helped you to grow in some way in your walk with God, if you are a non-believer looking for help, or if you are a new Christian, or a seasoned Christian. I believe that it has, because these words are not of my lips, but of my blessing.

CHAPTER 5

DEPRESSION OR DEMON?

I know it may not be an uncomfortable concept, but it has been placed on me to write this. Depression in the medical sense, is a state which brings great sorrow, and feelings of worthlessness. Feelings of failure, or not being good enough. The clinical description for depression is a complex mood disorder caused by various factors, including genetic predisposition, personality, stress and brain chemistry. Depression greatly affects the mood of a person. Depression is an evil sword of the Devil to control people and keep them down. This is absolutely a state of which God does not intend His children to be consumed with. He will turn all bad to be good for His glory, when any person repents and turns to God for healing.

In today's age, it seems there are more and more believers in Christ who are becoming depressed. I am not stating this to be the case in all circumstances, but I believe there is such a spiritual warfare going on at this time, that some believers of Christ are being tricked by the Devil to believe they have depression. They feel the symptoms, but instead of just feeling the deep sense of sorrow that most depressed people have, they often describe their depression to be a monster that is over-powering them, a force that is against them. Is this fact? Or is it speculation? I am not the one to judge, I am only here to write what God has placed upon me.

But I know truth in the reality, that in the end times, God's people will be tested, and tormented by the Devil, and so I believe strongly, that although the symptoms of depression may be very real, the actuality is that the Devil has released his demons to torment the souls of those believers who would have the most power against him. The demons torment the mind, and although they can confuse people to believe they are depressed, what they are really experiencing is a demon *chasing* them. Trying to get them to turn against God, trying to convince them to harm themselves, trying to tell them that they are not worthy, and that they are not loved.

I am not saying they are demon possessed, but maybe demon oppressed and are being stalked and tormented by a demon, for the sole purpose of stopping that person from fulfilling God's purpose in their life. See, God has big plans for His people, and some, He has chosen and given enormous plans, that would give the believer a great relationship with God, and they would be fulfilled in life and in spirit.

This doesn't mean the person would reach any amount of financial status, but maybe they would be doing work that would be making such a positive impact on their community that people would start turning their hearts to Jesus Christ, because they would be seeing His love through the person. This is just an example. But the truth is, the Devil is a liar and the father of lies. He is also selfish, and he wants all souls, but some, the bright stars, that God has planned to shine especially bright for His kingdom purposes, are those that the Devil sends his demons to chase, to try to get them to give up, to self-mutilate, or even so far as commit suicide, so that they lose their earthly heritage and God given purpose, and maybe their soul. It isn't where you came from, it is where you are going that counts.

Thanks be to God above, that these believers, who are experiencing anything like this, can rest in comfort and peace of knowing that they actually do have the power to make it stop, in the mighty name of Jesus. Discipline yourselves to pray, diligently, and it may take some time, but God will deliver you. (Remember, my depression took over 8 months to subside), but through that fight, through that battle, I found Jesus, who was, and is, my joy and strength. God was fighting for me, as he fights for all His children. Fight your battle on your knees, in prayer. Give the fight to God, tell Him that you need Him, that you are being chased, and you need Him, and use the name of Jesus Christ our Lord and Savior to cast the demon far from you. Plead the blood of Christ over your life daily and remember as long as you are a child of God, no harm will come to you, no matter how badly a demon will test you.

But you must remember, you are stronger, because you have God, and the God of your salvation is a BIG God, The Devil may be mighty, but God is Almighty and therefore, He is stronger than anything, and He can carry you through any trial. Remember to look for the lessons in the trial also. What gift did God give you that has been used to ward off the devil, but should have been used instead to just Glorify God while he fights the Devil's demons for you?

Remember the promises of God, stand on those promises in prayer, walk by faith and by the spirit and you will be redeemed, and God will give you peace in the fight. If you feel that you may be victim to the devils lies, and you recognize the demonic signs in your depressive state, my strong suggestion is to seek the face of God, and if you need help doing that, seek out a Christian Pastor to help you find the truth in your situation. Be aware of false prophets, be sure that the Pastor you are seeking advice from is a devout Christian, who has given his life to Jesus and is a true believer, who teaches that Jesus lived, died, and rose again for the remission of our sins, that we might be saved.

(NLT) Isaiah 43: 1 – 2 – But now, O Jacob, listen to the Lord who created you. O Israel, the one who formed you says, "do not be afraid, for I have ransomed you. I have called you by name; you are mine. (2) When you go through deep waters, I will be with you. When you go through rivers of difficulty, you will not drown. When you walk through the fire of oppression, you will not be burned up; the flames will not consume you. *II Timothy 1:7 –* For God has not given us a spirit of fear and timidity, but of power, love and self-discipline.

We continue now, in prayer. May God bless you in your struggles, as he blesses in your victory.

CHAPTER 6

POWER IN PRAYER.

D o not feel that you must close your eyes to pray. The Bible has provided us with numerous prayers to pray in times of need, sadness, happiness, thankfulness and the list goes on. Psalms alone is full of prayer. God's only requirement is that you are seeking after him with honesty, love, and a desire to know him personally. See, you can be a fan of Michael Jordan (I aimed for a popular name that most may know), you can know his stats, years he's played, when he started in business, the most popular of his current clothing lines, the list goes on… you can be a fan and know EVERY thing he has ever done, or ever written. You can even hang his poster on your wall. But until Michael Jordan invites you to his house for dinner, you will always be just an admirer, and not a friend. Much the same is with Jesus.

You can know everything there is to know about his walk on earth, maybe you can quote bible verses, never miss a Sunday service, even have a picture of Jesus hanging on the wall, but until you build a relationship with Jesus, and get to know him personally. You will never be invited to feast with him in the last days. Your RELATIONSHIP with Jesus, with our Father God will be what counts. Your good works cannot get you into heaven, neither will being able to quote the entire bible. (quoting the Bible is a blessing in itself though, I'm not taking from the importance of learning the word of God). I am however, stating, that you need to work on your relationship. Because the closer you draw to God, the more light enters your soul. The brighter your soul becomes, the more the darkness gets pushed out, and where there is no darkness, there can be no depression, or anxiety.

For when you give it all to God, He will create in you a new heart. And he will create in you a new spirit, and you will want to be God's best friend. See, people forget sometimes. God is more than just the almighty being that created the earth. God is our healer; he is the great physician. God is our counsellor, prince of peace. Our place of refuge. Any of this sound familiar to you? Where do you go, as a sinner, when you are depressed? To a doctor, to a counsellor, sometimes if the symptoms become severe enough, you go to a place of refuge, a rehabilitation home. Everything you need, you can find in Jesus. If you feel you have done too much to be forgiven, understand this, (NLT) Matthew 18: 21, 22 "Then Peter came to Him and asked, "Lord, how often should I forgive someone who sins against me? Seven times?" (22) "No, not seven times," Jesus replied, "but seventy times seven."

See Jesus will forgive us our mistakes, but once we ask for forgiveness and repent our sins, we need to be very intentional not to repeat those sins, because there is no forgiveness for intentional sinning. Jesus didn't die a horrible death on the cross so we could use forgiveness for our "be bad and get a free pass" card. We have to be earnest and honest in our desires. And when we discuss forgiving those who trespass against us. Yes, we are to forgive as Jesus does, however, we do not have to enter back into any dealings, or close relationship, but we do have to let the pain go, for our own growth, and if the person who trespassed against us, is asking genuine forgiveness, we also need to be responsible and intentional to consider the whole situation and be sure we do the right thing. Forgive, forget, move on, and rebuild is sometimes a big part of that healing. Depending on the relationship you are talking about. Rebuilding is so huge. Jesus has a desire to RESTORE, not reject.

So, before I get into the prayers that God has placed in my heart to write, I will start with this one: what one might call the sinner's prayer. And I implore you, if you are in the world, or new to Christ, or even if you are a lukewarm, cold or hot Christian in your walk with God. Read and PRAY this prayer earnestly, because ALL have sinned and come short of the glory of God. And none of us should be above asking forgiveness… one more time. And reach out to your local pastor of a Christian church for guidance on baptism. A very important step in becoming all you can be in Christ. Acts 2:38 Peter replied, "each of you must repent of our sins, and turn to God, and be baptized in the name of Jesus Christ for the forgiveness of your sins. Then you will receive the gift of the Holy Spirit."

Let us pray:

Dear God, I know that I am a sinner, and I have fallen short of your Glory and Grace. I have walked in the world and have found myself in a place of darkness, I ask your forgiveness for my sins, I believe that Jesus Christ is your Son, and that He died on the cross that I might be saved. You raised Him to life, and He resides in heaven with you until the day of your return for us. I want to trust Him as my Lord and Savior. From this day forward, guide my life, and help me to do your will. I pray this in Jesus name. Amen

(NLT)Philippians 4: 6-7: Do not be anxious about anything, but in every situation, through prayer and petition. With thanksgiving, present your requests to God, and the peace of God, which transcends all understanding, will guard your hearts and minds in Christ Jesus.

For if God is for you... who can be against you? Go forward in faith. Know that you are a child of God. And do not forget, sometimes God takes His time, because He has a beautiful plan for you. So, stay strong in your faith. The storm will pass. Also remember, the Devil will fight you harder, based on the size of the blessing God is trying to bestow into your life.

(NLT) Ephesians 6:10 – 20: A final word: Be strong in the Lord and in his mighty power. (11) Put on all of God's armor so that you will be able to stand firm against all strategies of the Devil. (12) For we are not fighting against flesh and blood enemies, but against evil rulers and authorities of the unseen world, against mighty powers in this dark world, and against evil spirits in the heavenly places.

(13) Therefore, put on every piece of God's armor so you will be able to resist the enemy in the time of evil. Then after the battle you will be standing firm. (14) Stand your ground, putting on the belt of truth and the body armor of God's righteousness. (15) For shoes, put on the peace that comes from the Good News so that you will be fully prepared (16) In addition to all of these, hold up the shield of faith to stop the fiery arrows of the

Devil (17) Put on salvation as your helmet and take the sword of the spirit, which is the word of God. (18) Pray in the spirit at all times and on every occasion. Stay alert and be persistent in your prayers for all believers everywhere. (19) And pray for me, too. Ask God to give me the right words so I can boldly explain God's mysterious plan that the Good News is for Jews and Gentiles alike. (20) I am in chains now, still preaching this message as God's ambassador. So, pray that I will keep on speaking boldly for him, as I should.

Pray diligently, with an open and honest heart. Seek after God. Stop praying and asking for everything all the time, God knows what you need, He knows everything about you! I know it feels better to say it out loud what is bothering you or what your needs are, and that's okay to do, but Pray with a heart of thanksgiving. In all moments, in the darkest moments of life when you feel you can't go on, Thank God for the air you breathe. Thank Him, for his mercy and grace is there, in our thanksgiving.

CHAPTER 7

PRAYERS FOR YOU

P ray any of these prayers, at any time, as often as you need to, read them out loud, in prayer, with honesty in your heart and a desire to better know the creator of the universe. (Critics, I hear you... I know, I know... you've been taught of the big bang, the theory of a loud noise bringing us into existence. Well, ponder this... What do you think it would sound like if God spoke in his full voice into space? Might be a little noisy... kind of like... a big bang. Just saying! ☺ You can keep your theories... I have the truth. With Love, through Jesus Christ. I hope that all that has been written has been received in love, to all readers.

Prayers for depression:

Dear Heavenly Father,

I come before you with a heavy heart. God you know my struggles, you know the darkness that is felt within me. God you know that when I breathe, it feels as though my breath is cutting the tubes of my lungs when my chest tightens with that pang of anxiety. God you know that I feel like I am alone when I have thousands of your people surrounding me.

Father, you know how cold I feel when I'm sweating from nervousness of having to show my face. This depression is a dark hallway with no glimmer of light, it is an empty room and I can't stand my own presence there.

God you know the peaks and valleys of this emotional overload, I am coming to you as a child of God, please Lord, remove me from this dark place. Bring me back into the light which you have placed within me. Lead me so that I can draw closer and closer to you Lord, I want to be free of the chains of depression that the devil has bound me in.

God, I pray that you will overtake my soul, God I give it all to you. I stand on your promises today Lord, so that in you I will find my rest. You are my healer and my savior, my redeemer and my friend. Jesus, I pray today Lord that you will go with me where ever I am, that you will go ahead of me and block the enemy from any further attacks on my spirit, and Lord that you will give me a new life in you.

Jesus, I know that the road is sometimes long and full of obstacles, but Lord, you are all powerful, and you have already won against Satan. You have made promises in your word Lord that you will never leave us nor forsake us. Jesus, I beg you Lord, that you will shine your light bright within my soul so that the darkness leaves me. Teach me Lord how to walk closer with you, teach me Lord how to pray. I ask in your precious and beautiful name today. Amen.

Dear Father in Heaven,

You know the struggles that I face daily, Lord, you know the hurt that I have deep down in my soul. God, I know that you are there, but you feel so very far away from me. Why is it that bad things are happening in my life? What is it that you want me to learn Father? I try so hard to just smile and go about my day, but Father, I feel like I am in a pit, and I feel like the walls are caving in. I don't know which way to turn! Father God, I pray that you will help me to see past the darkness, Lord, help me to see what it is you need me to know, so that I can step out of this darkness finally. God, I need you, every moment, every hour, every minute. I need to know that you are with me so that I can continue to fight this depression I am in. I need your power Lord, please send the Holy spirit to work within my soul Lord, to fill me with Light so that the darkness has no place to go. I Pray Father, that you will help me find my purpose. I love you Lord, and I pray that you will be with me while I sleep tonight, that you will give me comfort and send your angels to surround my home so that I can rest knowing they are protecting me from all evil thoughts, all evil actions and all things that the devil wants for my life. I thank you God for your blessings, I thank you for a place to sleep at night, even when I don't feel the safest. I thank you Lord for each moment of hope, each glimmer of a smile, each ounce of strength that I receive to have the effort to attempt being normal. I know Father that you have great things for my life. I know Father, that you are in control, even when I feel everything is out of control. Help me to take the right steps. I ask in your precious and beautiful name, the name of Jesus my Lord, and Savior, AMEN.

Dear Heavenly Father,

I thank you for this day, I thank you for your blessings in my life. I pray today Lord, that you will be with my friends and family that are suffering with depression and anxiety as I am suffering. I pray heavenly Father, that you will send an army of angels to fight the demons that are trying to over take their minds, and their lives, and their souls. I pray Father, that you will give each of them strength to get out of bed tomorrow, that you will give them a reason to smile tomorrow. I pray Father that you will be with them in every moment of sadness and darkness. Bring them a glimmer of light Father so that they can have a moment of peace, and in that moment of peace, Father, that they will see that you are the almighty healer of all things. That you Father, have the answer they are seeking to rid themselves of this depressive state. Bring back all the lost memories, from days that feel like fog, restore the hearts and the minds of each person that I love that suffers in near silence Father. I thank you for the lives of all my friends, and while I am asking for this for all of them, I also ask it for myself Father. I pray Lord that You will give me an experience of my own, that will help to strengthen my faith in You.

I thank you Father for this day, I thank you for all you are doing and all you have done. I ask all this in the name of Jesus Christ my Lord and Savior. Amen.

Prayer's for Anxiety

Dear Holy and Heavenly Father,

I come before you today with many issues, Jesus I come before You, knowing that You already see my struggles, you already know the hurt inside of me. Lord I pray today, that while I must go into the world and interact with people, that you will go before me, and ward off any of the triggers that may ignite my anxieties. Lord you know that the Devil has preplanned for me to feel like screaming on the inside all day long, while I must control and maintain my composure, that He will take any joy out of any circumstance I find myself in today.

Lord help me with things that should be making me happy, to cause mayhem inside of my body, so that any happiness that I could have felt is stripped from me.

Dear God, you know everything that happens inside of me, and I just pray Lord that you will step inside of my soul today, send your Holy Spirit to be upon me today God, protect me from my anxiety. Protect me from this gift of the Devil, because he only wants to keep me from the beautiful life that you have provided to me. I pray today Lord for your deliverance, in your time, your protection all the time. Let your will be done in my life, Amen.

Dear Father in Heaven,

I come to you today Lord with a heavy heart, a fast beating heart Father. I feel like I have lost control of myself, I feel I have lost control of my life. Lord, you see me when I am alone with my anxiety, you see how it knocks at my mind, it shakes my body, it trembles me and sets fear inside of me when I'm not looking. Paralyzing fear of nothing. I am afraid to talk to people, but I force myself and make a fool of my own actions, I am afraid to go out in public, but I go anyway, even though my feet feel like bricks, and my hands drip of sweat. Father, you know my struggle and my strife. I know that you are the answer I seek, and Father today I pray, that you will break the chains that bind my spirit. Father that I may be able to walk forward in life with no anxiety, that I can give you the Glory and all the praise forever for breaking this bondage in my life. I thank you Father for all you are doing, and all you have done. I know Heavenly Father, that you have broken chains before, and all that had to be done was to stand and walk… but heavenly Father, I don't know how to stand and walk on my own anymore, so I need some extra help. Please send your angels down to surround me in the moments I am consumed and pull me out of the pit of anxiety, Help grow my faith that You would have Your will done in my life, and I will be free from this bondage. I am losing air, I am drowning in a sea of falsified fears, lies of the devil. The devil has cast his snares of lies that I am aware are being told to my spirit, but the anxiety he has pressed inside of me is telling me to believe there is no hope. But Father, I know that in you, there is Hope, and in You Father, there is life. I trust you Lord, that even if it takes many days, that You will deliver me from this evil anxious spirit. For your love is everlasting, and I am done chasing answers in the world, and I am ready to chase after You. You left the 99 to chase me down, and I am here, asking you to teach me the way in which to go, so that the day will come, that the spirit of anxiety will surround me no longer. I thank you Lord for all you are doing in my life. I ask this in the precious and mighty name of Jesus Christ, my Lord and Savior. Amen.

A prayer for deliverance

Dear Heavenly and Holy Father;

I come before you today with a very heavy heart, and a deep sorrow.

Father God, I have been in a depressive state for a very long time, I have been tormented and torn from this shadow that follows me everywhere I go. Lord, I know that I am your child, and I know that I am covered by the blood of Jesus, but Lord, I need help right now. Lord, you know everything, you know every situation and every heartache, Father you know what I have been enduring, and Father only you can tell if what I am feeling are the effects of depression of the mind, or the torturous lies of the Devil's demons against me. Father, I know that these demons cannot penetrate my soul Lord, because my soul belongs to you.

Father they can scratch at the surface, and make me feel these terrible feelings, make me feel that I'm losing my mind, and draining my energy so that I fall far from your will and purpose in my life. Father God I pray today, that the Holy Spirit and fire will fill my soul Father. That by the name of Jesus Christ, the King of King's and Lord of Lord's that any demon of Satan that is trying to get close to my soul, that is trying to overcome my mind and my emotions Lord, that it be cast far from me in the name of Jesus, by the blood of Jesus. Father God I will pray this prayer diligently until I see the cloud of darkness lift from my life, Father God I will praise you even in the times of darkness.

Father God I love you and I thank you for my life, Father I thank you for my struggles, for in times of struggle Lord, you teach me how to be humble, Father you teach me how to be thankful for your Grace and your mercy. Father I pray today,

Father that you will be with me all of my days. Thank you, Father, for your word. Thank you, Lord, for your love, and for sending your Son, Jesus to die for my sins so that I do not have to endure an eternity of torture. I ask in your precious and beautiful name. I claim the promises of your word upon my life today Father. I raise Hallelujah to you Father.

Amen.

For those of you searching for more on depression and its evil influences and are wondering about the original prayer that started me on this path (told about in the first chapter), the very prayer given to me by God to bless the heart of another person. I am copy and pasting it into this book, as a reminder of the POWER of Jesus. This prayer was originally meant for one man, but by sharing it, it may inspire and help others. It is only right to include it here. The beautiful words that God gave directly to me, for the help of someone else. It's amazing how God can use us, when we LET HIM DO HIS JOB! Sorry... I had to make sure you caught that! I also became very aware in this prayer, God opened my eyes to the way I pray. Never before this moment that the prayer was given to me, had I ever prayed acknowledging God as my Father in such a way as this. This particular prayer was the exact words that GOD used to give to someone who needed an exact prayer for their life. Because as humans, we sometimes want to pray, but we don't know how. We stumble over our words, or we just decide to stay quiet because we just don't know what to say. I know that God can hear the cry of our hearts, but sometimes, He commands us to take a stand for our faith and take a step to our healing. In this particular case, God gave the words. And I did not change any of it to suit grammar, or most punctuation because I wanted it to be authentic, to the original. I also want it to be readable to all people. So please forgive the mistakes within this prayer but enjoy the power within it. Blessings to you all!

Prayer for Depression

Dear Heavenly Father, healer, and friend,

I pray to you at this moment for the deep dark battle I am facing. Father God you already know the details, Lord, you see the suffering within me. The strong hold that the enemy has over my mind and my heart today Father.

Jesus, I come to you in reverence, asking first forgiveness for all I have done, and all I have failed to do. Father God, I pray that you will stretch your loving arms down and wrap them around my soul today. I believe Jesus, that you died for my sins to be covered, and for my hope and future, I thank you father for your sacrifice so that I may be saved, and father I thank you for your healing power. I place the darkest parts of my soul and mind in your hands father God, because Lord you are the light of the world. Father God you have already won against Satan. He has no power here in this place.

Father God, Satan has no power in my heart or in my mind or my emotions. Father God, I cast any of Satan's demons far from me in the name of Jesus. Father God I cast Satan far from me in the precious name of Jesus. I thank you today father God for your healing power. I thank you today Jesus for removing this burden from my soul father. Jesus, I thank you for your precious healing power and I praise you for your glory.

Jesus, I need you to send your Holy Spirit and fire into my soul Father. So that I may feel your presence near. Father God I thank you today for all of the blessings in my life Father. I thank you Father for my family father, I thank you for my home Father, for the air I breathe Father, for waking me up each day and giving me just enough strength dear Father to get to this moment Father.

Father God In you I place my trust, Father God in you I find my rest. Father God in you I find my healing, Father God in you I find peace.

Today Father God I pray and believe that you will cast out all the darkness from me.

Father God I know the devil doesn't want to let me go, I know father that Satan wants to keep me in his grasp. Father, but by the power of Jesus, by the blood spilled on the cross for my sin and transgressions, by the word that you promised Father, I command Satan to be cast far from me Father. I know he is angry and will try to attack me Father, but I fear not because you Father are with me. You, Father are in control and you Father, have all the power here. Father God I thank you for your deliverance, Father I thank you for your kindness and mercy. You are my refuge and my strength Father God. I am your child Father God, and you have promised in your word that if I repent and turn to you Father that I will be born again, and Father I know and I believe that you have cleansed me of all past transgressions. Father do a work in me.

Father I have suffered much despair Father, and I have lost time Father God, I have felt clawing at my soul Father, and I have felt loneliness in the most crowded of places Father, you know all my secrets Father, you know my deepest wounds Father God. I ask Father that you flood my heart, soul and mind with light Father God. Because Satan and his demons cannot survive in the light. The tricks of the devil cannot take root in the light. Only the dark places Father, so I plead Father for your help, I beg for your mercy father as I am not worthy on my own but only by the blood of Jesus. You are the way the truth and the life Father, and although the devil tries to tell me every moment that I am not worthy of grace, Father I know, and I believe Father that I am worthy because of your saving and healing power Father God.

Jesus as I read, I feel that I am a fraud to pray this prayer. Because the Devil fights me on every angle. Father but I know that these words are directly from you Father, because Father

God you know that I don't have the words Father, you know that I am lacking strength Father, you know I feel discouraged and down Father. You know my every thought. The inner workings of my mind, so Father I thank you for sending me this prayer Father. I thank you in the name of Jesus for meeting my needs. Father God I praise you Father for all you do. Father God I thank you Father for reminding me that all I need is you, that I can let go of all my fears, anxieties and all of my control. Father and I am safe with you. For Father, you see my future, and through your power you can make beauty from even my darkness. There is a work Father that you have for me Father and I will pray this prayer Father, daily, Father as a tribute of my faith in you Father God.

I thank you Father for your mercy and Grace. Father I thank you for all your blessings Father. I thank you Father for your word, and I stand today on the promises of God. James 4:7, says, so humble yourselves before God. Resist the devil, and he will flee from you. Come close to God, and God will come close to you. Wash your hands you sinners, purify your hearts, for your loyalty is divided between God and the world.

James 4:10. Humble yourselves before the Lord, and He will lift you up in honor.

Father I thank you this day, Father God I thank you this moment for knowing I have suffered and that I need you Father God. For you are Holy and if the stars are made to worship so will I Father God.

I will praise and worship your Holy name. I thank you Father for your love and your mercy upon me Father God. I praise you for your power and influence Father God. I praise you for your healing power and strength for me. I am not worthy in the flesh Father God, but in spirit and in truth.

I thank you Father for all you have done, and for all you are doing Father God. I thank you Father for sending your son, Father I thank you for sending your Holy Spirit. Father I thank you for the hedge of protection you are placing around me Father, I thank you Father for you are all knowing. You are my friend, you are my comfort, my peace and my hope for a future. In You, all things are possible and in You all things are made new.

I thank you Father God for your mercy upon my life. I thank you Father God for your love that will fill my soul until it flows through my pores Father, so I am a light for you Father. My existence is because of You Father. You knew my purpose before I was born, and Father I want you to redefine me. Refine me and make me into who I am supposed to be for You Father. I know it isn't too late Father God, for in you all things are possible. In You I hold my trust. In You Father I place my life. Take control Father, as only you can.

I pray in your precious and holy name, with a humble heart, your child raises a hallelujah, and Amen.

To the few and to the many, our help comes from the Lord, God almighty. May his will be done, even upon the end times in which we live. God's word is a living word. (NLT) Jeremiah 29: 11-13 "For I know the plans I have for you," says the Lord. "They are plans for good and not for disaster, to give you a future and a hope." (12) in those days when you pray, I will listen. (13) If you look for me wholeheartedly, you will find me."

May God bless everyone who earnestly seeks HIM through Jesus Christ his son!

I have so much more I could say, but I feel this is enough for now. I need to once again seek the face of God, so that He can guide me on the next journey of writing. I know that God has blessed me in a way that I can reach many for His Glory. Not everyone will receive this with open arms, not everyone will appreciate the journey, or the words within these precious pages. But I thank God, for his grace, and I thank God for trusting me to write this manuscript, to send this seed out into the world. I pray it grows, as a strong oak tree grows from a tiny seed, they both look so different on the outside, but on the inside… it's just amazing how once that seed is placed deep in the darkness of the ground… how the roots have to take hold, and soak up the moisture in order to start birthing the feeble trunk of a tree… and with time and patience, the years bring on the rings, that will then help it to grow in size and strength. How much is this like the Christian walk? Most people turn to God in their darkness, but if they hold on, and soak up God's word, and soak up the lessons, even in the most difficult of moments, oh how beautiful it is, when the people see the light, and they raise up and build strength in and through Jesus. I thank God for his mercy on my life. I thank God, for planting me, for stretching me and trusting me to do the work only God could call me to do.

Before I close this book with these last few words, I have a prayer of my own:

Heavenly Father,

I thank you for loving me and giving me a heart of burden for all the people on this earth, for all of your beautiful children, that I was chosen by you, to write the content within this book Lord. You have taught me so much, and. You are still teaching me. And I thank you for ALL of the lessons. Especially for the lessons that do not make sense to anyone else, because it is in those heavenly times, that I see you so clearly. I thank You LORD for your blessing on me. I pray that as these words go to print, that your protection will be around them, that Your name will be HONORED and Praised for all you have done by the people that read this book. Father, I pray, that each soul that is stirred, and each spirit of depression and anxiety that pulls in fear, that You Father, will take control, that you will show yourself to each person, and that the spirits of anxiety and depression will be cast from the hearts and lives of all who call on your name, believe you are God, ask for forgiveness and seek your face as I have. I thank you God, for showing me the path to righteousness, and I thank you Father, for helping me when I stumble and fall. Lord You are my everything, and in all things, I give you all the praise, and glory. For without You in my life, I am nothing. I have learned the lesson I have taught many times… seek the things you wish to find, if I want to find love and kindness, goodness, mercy and grace, it is there for me (and anyone else who desires it). Seek it in ALL I do, in what I search online, in the books I read, in my conversations, in my relationships. Lord, in all things, I seek You. I thank you again for building my humble spirit, and I thank you for walking me through my own dark valleys. I put all of my faith, and trust, in You. I ask your protection, conviction, and love for all who have read this book. I pray it blesses their lives immensely. Amen.

Bible Verse Notations: NLT = New Living Translation, Illustrated Study Bible.

9 781728 339160